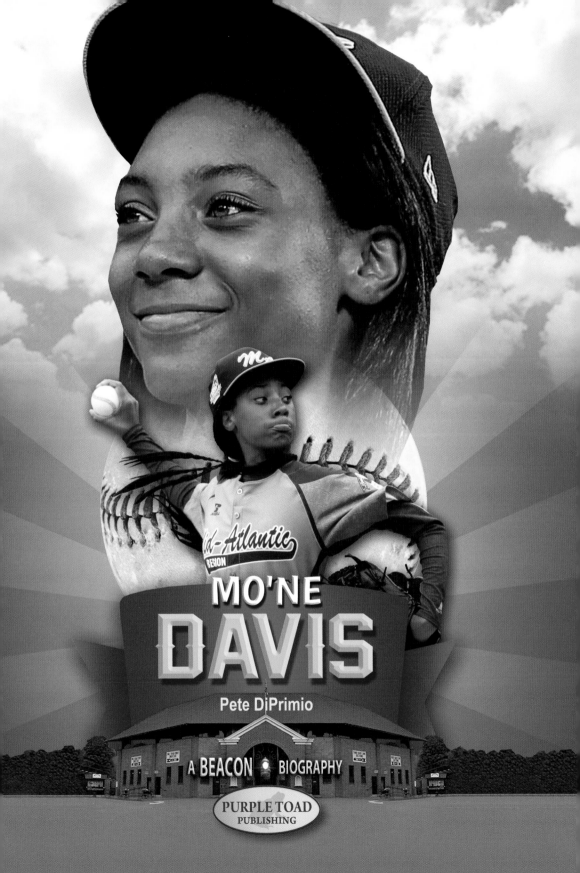

MO'NE
DAVIS

Pete DiPrimio

A BEACON ◆ BIOGRAPHY

PURPLE TOAD
PUBLISHING

PURPLE TOAD
PUBLISHING

Printing   1   2   3   4   5   6   7   8   9

A Beacon Biography

Angelina Jolie
Big Time Rush
Carly Rae Jepsen
Drake
Ed Sheeran
Harry Styles of One Direction
Jennifer Lawrence
Kevin Durant
Lorde
Malala
Markus "Notch" Persson, Creator of Minecraft
Mo'ne Davis
Muhammad Ali
Neil deGrasse Tyson
Peyton Manning
Robert Griffin III (RG3)

Publisher's Cataloging-in-Publication Data
DiPrimio, Pete.
  Mo'Ne Davis / written by Pete DiPrimio.
    p. cm.
          Includes bibliographic references and index.
          ISBN 9781624691898
1. Davis, Mo'Ne. 2. Baseball players—United States—Biography—Juvenile literature. 3. Little League Baseball, Inc.—Juvenile literature. I. Series: Beacon Biographies Collection Two.
  GV865 2016
  796.357

Library of Congress Control Number: 2015941815

eBook ISBN: 9781624691904

ABOUT THE AUTHOR: Pete DiPrimio is an award-winning sportswriter for the *Fort Wayne [Indiana] News-Sentinel,* and a longtime freelance writer. He's been an adjunct lecturer for the National Sports Journalism Center at IUPU-Indianapolis and for Indiana University's School of Journalism. He is the author of three nonfiction books pertaining to Indiana University athletics, and more than 15 children's books. He is currently completing his first novel. Pete is also a fitness instructor, plus a tennis and racquetball enthusiast.

PUBLISHER'S NOTE: The data in this book has been researched in depth, and to the best of our knowledge is factual. Although every measure is taken to give an accurate account, Purple Toad Publishing makes no warranty of the accuracy of the information and is not liable for damages caused by inaccuracies. This story has not been authorized or endorsed by Mo'Ne Davis.

CONTENTS

Chapter One
The High Road 5

Chapter Two
Seeing is Believing 9

Chapter Three
Shining in the Spotlight 13

Chapter Four
Back to a New Normal 19

Chapter Five
Poise and Perspective 23

Further Reading 28

Books 28

Works Consulted 28

On the Internet 30

Glossary 30

Index 32

Mo'ne Davis shows the form that enabled her to become the first girl to pitch a shutout and earn a victory in the Little League World Series.

Mo'ne Davis took the high road. She forgave when others might have struck back.

This Philadelphia teenager had won awards and glory rarely given to a 13-year-old. *Sports Illustrated* had honored her as its SportsKid of the Year, and it made her the first Little League player ever to be on its cover. The right-hander with the trademark braids had dominated in Little League World Series play with a 70-mph fastball that rivaled the form of Major League Baseball pitchers—in a sport that might not even be her best.

And yet, when a college baseball player from Bloomsburg University in Pennsylvania tweeted a crude remark about her that got him kicked off the team in the winter of 2015, Mo'ne responded with kindness and understanding.

She emailed the president of Bloomsburg, asking that first baseman Joey Casselberry be allowed to return to the team. She wrote that he had just made a mistake, as everybody does.

"Why not give him a second chance?" she asked.

Casselberry had heard that Disney was thinking about making a movie about Mo'ne and her amazing accomplishments. The movie would highlight her as the first female to throw a

Bloomsburg University baseball player Joey Casselberry's crude tweet about Mo'ne got him kicked off the team.

shutout in Little League World Series play. A few days later, her team lost to a squad from Las Vegas, Nevada.

Casselberry got himself in trouble with this tweet: "Disney is making a movie about Mo'ne Davis? WHAT A JOKE. [She] got rocked by Nevada."

Bloomsburg officials were quick to act. They kicked him off the team, saying they were "deeply saddened" by Casselberry's words, which "do not represent us."

According to *TMZ Sports,* Bloomsburg President David L. Soltz said that while he respected Mo'ne's opinion and praised her maturity, he would not let Casselberry return to the team.

Later, Mo'ne told *SI Now* that she doesn't let what people say on social media, such as Twitter, bother her.

"A lot of people just want attention," she told *SI Now.* "They just want to see how you react, so they can put it up on their social media so they can make it seem like you're the bad person, and you're not."

An honor roll student with a dream to play college and professional basketball, Mo'ne showed poise, leadership, and class beyond her years. She has shown that inner city sports teams can have big-picture dreams because those dreams sometimes do come true. She offers hope when others see hopelessness. She brings inspiration to those who struggle to find it.

It's for those reasons, and so much more, that she has such a bright future.

Mo'ne showed kindness and understanding beyond her years in forgiving Joey Casselberry. Those are among the qualities that make her such a special person.

Mo'ne doesn't pitch the way people think a girl can pitch, or hit like one. She makes an impact every time she steps on a baseball field.

Seeing is Believing

Mo'ne Ikea Davis was born on June 24, 2001, in Philadelphia, Pennsylvania, to Lamar Davis and Lakeisha McLean. By the time she was six, she was living with Lakeisha and her stepfather, Mark Williams. She was an ordinary girl doing some extraordinary things. Few people noticed—until a year later.

Steve Bandura, the Anderson Monarchs youth baseball coach, helped see to that.

In the fall of 2008, Bandura raced a setting sun on a tractor. He was grooming the Marian Anderson Recreational Center's baseball field in South Philadelphia for another game. The fall season was coming to an end, and he was getting ready to coach a youth basketball team. He saw a group of kids throwing a football around in left field—all boys except for one girl. She was throwing spirals to rival NFL quarterback Peyton Manning.

It was Mo'ne Davis, the cousin of one of his players.

"I'm watching her throw perfect spirals every single time," Bandura told Sara Baicker of CSNPhilly.com, "and throwing them a good distance. I was like, 'What is that?'"

Anderson Monarchs coach Steve Bandura (top right) has a history of finding and developing good youth baseball players.

Bandura had to find out, so he invited her to practice with his boys' basketball team. Not only did she show up, she thrived—even though she had never played organized basketball before. She'd never seen drills, such as the three-player weave the team was doing. This drill involves a series of passes and cuts that ends with a layup. Bandura suggested she watch, but instead she got in line. She hadn't come to watch.

"I watched her eyes study what was going on and process it," Bandura told Baicker. "On her turn, she did it like she was doing it her whole life. That's when I knew. You could tell she had the athleticism, but that analytical skill, you just can't teach that."

Mo'ne thrived in basketball, baseball, and soccer—all against boys, some older, almost all bigger. Bandura, who has had pitchers reach the minor leagues, said she was the best pitcher he's ever had.

Springside Chestnut Hill Academy, one of the top schools in Philadelphia

Bandura and others helped Mo'ne transfer to Springside Chestnut Hill Academy, a highly regarded private girls' school in Philadelphia. It was more than an hour away from her southwest Philadelphia home, but the time and effort paid off. Mo'ne did just as well in the classroom as she did on the sports fields, making the honor roll.

Mo'ne continued to do well and joined the Taney (TAW-nee) Dragons Little League baseball team. The buzz grew around Philadelphia about a girl who could out-do boys, but things really took off on August 10, 2014. That is when she pitched Taney into the Little League World Series. Her three-hit shutout in an 8–0 win over Newark, New Jersey, got national attention.

"She was in control from start to finish," Newark manager Tim Bush told the Philadelphia *Daily News.* "She was great."

The Little League World Series has been held since 1947 in Williamsport, Pennsylvania. Sixteen teams from all over the world compete in it. Mo'ne had success against a team from Delaware, and against others in the Philadelphia area. But people wondered, could a girl succeed against the best boys' teams and players of her age in the world?

They were about to find out.

Even under the brightest spotlights, Mo'ne keeps her poise and concentration.

Shining in
the Spotlight

The pressure grew under bright sunshine in Williamsport, and Mo'ne didn't blink.

Two months past her thirteenth birthday, a few weeks before she started the eighth grade, a nation watched. Little League World Series television ratings soared to record highs for networks ESPN and ABC. Mo'ne's hometown newspaper, the *Philadelphia Inquirer*, put her on the front page for five straight days in August.

Sports Illustrated made Mo'ne the first Little League player ever to make its cover. The headline declared: "Mo'ne: Remember Her Name (As If We Could Ever Forget)." She was just the fourth American girl to play in the World Series (only 18 girls have made it worldwide), and the first since 2004.

Some might have wilted in the spotlight.

Mo'ne shone.

On Friday afternoon, August 15, Mo'ne strode to the Lamade Stadium mound, all 5'4" and 111 pounds of her. Her traditional hit-the-field song, Beyoncé's "Run the World (Girls)," played in the background. Her long dark braids swayed from her

The flying braids of Mo'ne Davis signal another blazing pitch is 56 feet, 6 inches away and coming up fast on the hitter.

burgundy baseball cap down to her waist. She was calm in her blue jersey with burgundy trim and white baseball pants. And she stayed calm as she threw 70-mph heat few hitters could catch up to.

There was a reason for that. The Little League pitching mound is 14 feet closer to home plate than it is in the major leagues. A 70-mph fastball there is like a 91-mph fastball in the majors. (The average Little League pitcher's fastball is 50 mph.)

"Throwing 70 miles an hour—THAT's throwing like a girl," Mo'ne told CBS News.

How can someone so small throw so hard?

ESPN's John Brenkus used a video to show Mo'ne's great pitching form. Her delivery is consistent, and she has something called kinetic linking. This basically means she puts her whole body behind every pitch. Her throwing motion is similar to Philadelphia Phillies relief pitcher Jonathan Papelbon's.

Add that to a fierce competitiveness (she has a glare that could freeze a grizzly at 20 yards) and mental toughness beyond her years. It's no wonder Taney Dragons manager Alex Rice told *CBS News*, "You won't see her fall apart on the mound. You can't get to her. It's a real poised group, and she's at the head of it."

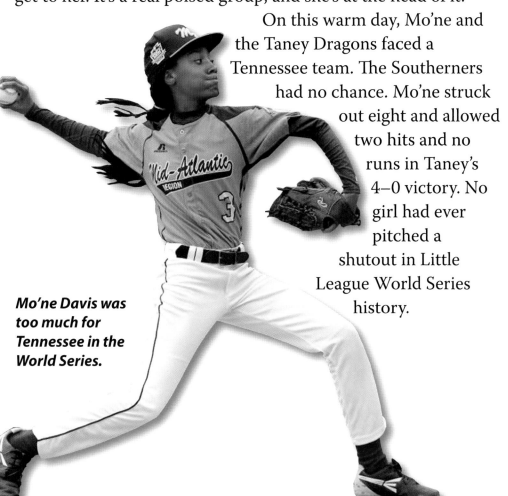

On this warm day, Mo'ne and the Taney Dragons faced a Tennessee team. The Southerners had no chance. Mo'ne struck out eight and allowed two hits and no runs in Taney's 4–0 victory. No girl had ever pitched a shutout in Little League World Series history.

Mo'ne Davis was too much for Tennessee in the World Series.

"It's the Mo Show out there," Rice told *The New York Times*.

The country couldn't get enough. Even professional superstars noticed.

Pittsburgh Pirates center fielder Andrew McCutchen tweeted, "S/O [Shout Out] to PA and @MoNeDavis11. Rooting for u guys over here!"

California Angels star Mike Trout tweeted, "Mo'ne Davis is straight dominating . . . fun to watch!!!"

NBA scoring champ Kevin Durant tweeted, "This youngster is striking everybody out and she is a girl. I love it."

A few days later, in a win over Pearland, Texas, Mo'ne had a run-scoring single, making her just the sixth girl to get a hit in Little League World Series history.

Texas found out in the World Series that Mo'ne can hurt you with her bat as well as her arm.

Mo'ne was so popular at the Little League World Series facilities that people swarmed her for autographs. Officials drove her to and from the games in a golf cart. This service gave her some privacy and protected her from fans who couldn't seem to get enough of her.

She was so famous everybody knew her by her first name—like a rock star or a movie star or a pro athlete.

George Washington University professor Mark Hyman talked to Jer'e Longman of *The New York Times.* He said that, during the 2014 Little League World Series, Mo'ne was "the most talked-about baseball player on earth." He also said, "More people are talking about her than [superstar New York Yankees baseball player] Derek Jeter."

Signs popped up in the Lamade Stadium stands that said, "Show me the Mo'ne."

Through it all, Mo'ne kept her calm and her perspective with these main goals: "Hitting homers and striking boys out," she told *TODAY.*

On August 20, 2014, under the lights and with a record-breaking audience watching on ESPN, Mo'ne finally met her match in a power hitting Las Vegas team. In 2 1/3 innings she gave up three runs, striking out six and walking one. Taney lost 8–1.

No matter. Mo'ne helped to change the way people think about girls—and women—in sports. She had become a role model for the 21st century.

Not bad for a 13-year-old.

Mo'ne's World Series success helped her meet NBA superstar Stephen Curry (top) and make an appearance on NBC's The Tonight Show Starring Jimmy Fallon.

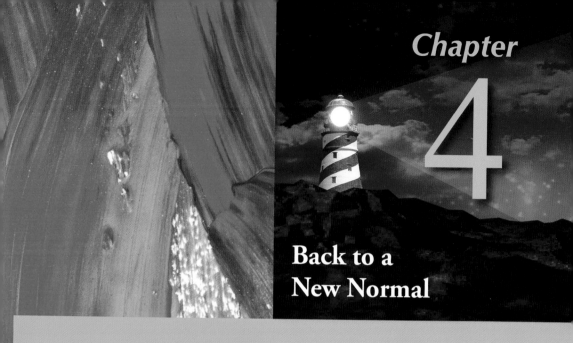

What do you do after capturing the nation's attention?

For Mo'ne, it was racing around the country on a whirlwind tour before going back to school.

She was invited to the WNBA's annual honors luncheon in New York City. While there, she also appeared on NBC's *The Tonight Show Starring Jimmy Fallon.* Fallon bet her that she couldn't strike him out. The winner would get a cheese steak, one of the favorite foods in her home city of Philadelphia.

With Dragons catcher Scott Bandura catching, Mo'ne threw 10 times. She struck out Fallon. And Fallon paid his bet.

Mo'ne then went to the WNBA conference finals in Minnesota. There she met such famous players as Brittney Griner, Diana Taurasi, and Maya Moore. She flew to Los Angeles to throw out the first pitch between the Dodgers and the Washington Nationals. She met Dodgers superstar pitcher and Cy Young Award winner Clayton Kershaw.

"It was really cool to meet him," she told AP.

Mo'ne even got a call from University of Connecticut women's basketball coach Geno Auriemma. By the summer of 2015, this coach had won 10 national championships. He tied former UCLA men's coach

John Wooden for the most college basketball titles ever. Mo'ne says she would like to play basketball for Connecticut, and then in the WNBA.

Mo'ne told the Associated Press they had only talked about the Little League World Series. ("He just congratulated me," she said.) Even so, the NCAA found that Auriemma had broken the rules on recruiting. Coaches may contact players only at certain times. Auriemma's call came during a non-contact period.

Mo'ne told the Associated Press she was "sad" Auriemma was penalized.

Finally, it was time to return to a normal life.

"I'm happy to be going back home and seeing my friends and just being Mo'ne," she said.

This was a new normal.

In October 2014, Mo'ne was in a 16-minute documentary about her accomplishments, called, "I Throw Like a Girl." It was directed by Spike Lee, one of the most famous directors in the world. She also donated the No. 3 jersey she wore in the Little League World Series to Major League Baseball's Hall of Fame in Cooperstown, New York. And she threw out the ceremonial first pitch for Game 4 of Major League Baseball's World Series in San Francisco.

The next month she and her Taney Dragons were part of the annual Macy's Thanksgiving Day Parade in New York City.

Mo'ne also joined shoe company M4D3 (Make A Difference Everyday) to design sneakers for girls. Some of the money would go to Plan International's Because I Am a Girl. This charity helps millions of girls in the developing world rise out of poverty.

"I never thought at the age of 13 I'd be a role model, but having young girls look up to me is pretty cool!" Mo'ne said through M4D3's Instagram account.

In December 2014, *Sports Illustrated Kids* named her its SportsKid of the Year. That impressed First Lady Michelle Obama. She tweeted

Mo'ne's success impressed Michelle Obama, the First Lady. Here Mo'ne helps her read 'Twas the Night Before Christmas *during the annual Christmas tree lighting ceremony in Washington, DC, in December 2014.*

her congratulations, saying, "You knocked it out of the park for girls everywhere."

Time magazine agreed. It listed Mo'ne among the 25 most influential teens of 2014.

In addition, Mo'ne and author Hilary Beard wrote a book about her life, *Mo'ne Davis: Remember My Name.* It was released in March 2015 by HarperCollins Children's Books.

In a statement from HarperCollins, Mo'ne said, "When I joined an all-boys baseball team, my mom wasn't too happy. I proved to her (and to me) that I could do anything I set my mind to. I'm just a girl that likes to play sports and I'm excited to share my story with everyone. I hope it encourages people to take a chance and play the sports they want to play and not just the ones people expect them to play."

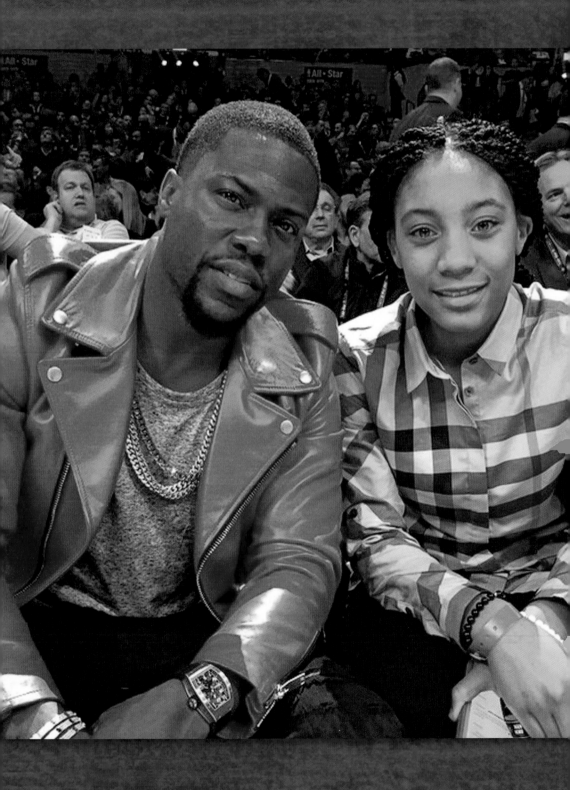

Mo'ne played nice with comedian and movie star Kevin Hart before outscoring him on the basketball court.

Poise and Perspective

Comedian and movie star Kevin Hart had had enough. He'd handled the pressure of making movies and getting thousands of people to laugh during nightly comedy shows. He had survived televised basketball pressure to win four MVP awards from the NBA's Celebrity All-Star Game.

But when Mo'ne burned him with a knee-buckling spin move to drive to the basket and score in the All-Star game of 2015, Hart knew the time had come. He said he's retiring from any more celebrity basketball games. He jokingly blamed Mo'ne.

"That little girl embarrassed me on live television," Hart said on *The Jim Rome Show.* "It's only going to get worse if I keep going back. I don't want to see what's going to happen next."

"I'm officially retired from the Celebrity All-Star Game. I can't do it anymore. I've done all there is to do. My kids are happy, they feel like their dad went out on top. I think if I go back, it's only going to get worse, I can't go down, I can only go up, and I left with a bang. I did what all the greats say you should do."

He joked with Rome that Mo'ne was more like Super Girl than an ordinary teenager.

Kevin Hart thought he had Mo'ne right where he wanted her while playing defense during an All-Star basketball game. He was wrong.

"Basically, any 13-year-old girl that can throw an 80-mile-per-hour fastball, something is wrong. I want her checked. . . . The girl's too good."

Mo'ne's Little League success could have made her rich—if she wanted to give up playing college sports.

USA Today reported that, according to an owner of a sports memorabilia company, Mo'ne could have made a lot of money just for her autograph. She could have earned between $25,000 and $100,000 by signing 500 to 1,000 items such as baseballs, drinking cups, and shirts during the Little League World Series. And there could have been a lot more deals like that.

But making that money would have violated NCAA rules. Earning money from sports makes a person a professional. Professionals cannot play college sports. That would be a big problem, because Mo'ne wants to play in college—and beyond.

Still, others were making money from Mo'ne's fame. *USA Today* reported that a baseball supposedly autographed by her was sold on eBay. Bidding started at $199 and reached $500.

About 40 autographed items were sold overall. Companies made Mo'ne jerseys and tried to sell them on Facebook.

Mo'ne uses her fame to help others. She has her own line of sneakers to benefit Plan International's "Because I am a Girl" charity which helps young, poverty-stricken girls.

The Internet and web sites such as eBay make it easy for people to sell memorabilia. Little League officials were unhappy about it, but said there was no way to stop it. All they could do was try to limit the autographs so that they were just for kids, and not for adults.

Meanwhile, interest in baseball, especially from inner city parents, grew, thanks to Mo'ne. One parent called Taney officials about a tryout for her daughter.

The daughter was three years old.

Through it all, Mo'ne has kept her poise and perspective.

"No matter who you are, you should be able to do what you like to do and what you've always dreamed of doing."

Yes, the future is bright for Mo'ne Davis.

In June of 2015, on the day before her 14th birthday, Mo'ne was drafted by the world-renowned Harlem Globetrotters basketball team. They used what is called a "Future Discovery Clause" to buy the rights to Davis when she graduates from college. Mo'ne is just the third female ever to be drafted to the Harlem Globetrotters.

In July, 2015, Davis won the "Best Breakthrough Athlete" award at the ESPYs in Los Angeles.

Books

Davis, Mo'ne, and Hilary Beard. *Mo'ne Davis: Remember My Name: My Story from First Pitch to Game Changer.* New York: HarperCollins, 2015.

Verrick, Audrey. *She Loved Baseball: The Effa Manley Story.* New York: Balzer + Bray, 2010.

Works Consulted

"The 25 Most Influential Teens of 2014." *Time,* October 13, 2014. http://time.com/3486048/most-influential-teens-2014/

Associated Press. "Baseball by the Book: Mo'ne Davis Memoir Coming Next March." November 17, 2014.

Baicker, Sara. CSNPhilly.com. "Coach Discovered Mo'ne Davis – Playing Football." August 12, 2014. http://www.csnphilly.com/baseball-llws/coach-discovered-mone-davis-%E2%80%94-playing-football

Brenkus, John. ESPN Video: "Sport Science – Mo'ne Davis." http://espn.go.com/espnw/video/11352094/mone-davis

Chen, Albert. "Mo'ne Davis, Taney Take Center Stage at Little League World Series." *Sports Illustrated,* August 20, 2014. http://www.si.com/more-sports/2014/08/20/mone-davis-taney-little-league-world-series

Clements, Erin. "Little League star Mo'ne Davis designs sneaker line to benefit impoverished girls." *Today News,* March 18, 2015. http://www.today.com/news/little-league-star-mone-davis-designs-sneaker-line-benefit-impoverished-t9706

ESPN.com: "Mo'ne Davis Is Sports Kid of the Year." December 1, 2014. http://espn.go.com/sports/llws14/story/_/id/11962772/mone-davis-named-sports-illustrated-sports-kid-year

Kim, Eun Kyung. *Today.* "Little League Pitching Phenom Mo'ne Davis Strikes a Chord on *Sports Illustrated* Cover." August 20, 2014, *Today News.* http://www.today.com/news/little-league-pitcher-mone-davis-makes-cover-sports-illustrated-1D80087783

Lipinsky, Tara. "Meet Mo'Ne Davis, The Girl Who Pitched Her Team Into the LLWS." CBS Pittsburgh, August 12, 2014. http://pittsburgh.cbslocal.com/2014/08/12/meet-mone-davis-the-girl-who-pitched-her-team-into-the-llws/

Little League World Series Results, 2014. http://www.llbws.org/media/
news/Westwinsgame24.htm

Longman, Jere. "Mo'ne Davis Takes Little League World Series Stardom in
Stride." *The New York Times,* August 19, 2014. http://www.nytimes.
com/2014/08/20/sports/baseball/mone-davis-takes-little-league-world-
series-stardom-in-stride.html?_r=0

"Mo'ne Davis Becomes First Girl to Throw a Shutout in LLWS." *Sports
Illustrated.* August 15, 2014. http://www.si.com/more-
sports/2014/08/15/mone-davis-shutout-little-league-world-series

"Mo'ne on Abusive Tweeter: Everyone Deserves a Second Chance." *SI.com,*
March 24, 2015. http://www.si.com/more-sports/2015/03/24/mone-
davis-twitter-college-baseball-player-bloomsburg-university

Murray, Elizabeth. "Little League Star Mo'ne Davis Strikes out Jimmy Fallon
on 'Tonight Show.'" *TODAY,* September 6, 2014. http://www.today.com/
popculture/little-league-star-mone-davis-strikes-out-jimmy-fallon-
tonight-1D80128722

Peter, Josh. "Mo'ne Davis Merchandise Means Money—and Outrage." *USA
TODAY Sports,* August 22, 2014. http://www.usatoday.com/story/
sports/2014/08/20/mone-davis-little-league-world-series-
autograph/14352429/

Tauber, Michelle. "Mo'ne Davis: 5 Things to Know About the History-
Making Little League Pitcher." *People,* August 17, 2014. http://www.
people.com/article/mone-davis-little-league-philadelphia-taney-
dragons

Vecenie, Sam. "Kevin Hart Retires from Celebrity Game, Cites Mo'ne Davis
as Reason." *CBS Sports,* February 19, 2015. http://www.cbssports.com/
nba/eye-on-basketball/25073990/kevin-hart-retires-from-celebrity-
game-cites-mone-davis-as-reason

On the Internet

Moro, Paul. "The Girl Who Struck Out Babe Ruth." *Featury.* May 20, 2008.
http://umpbump.com/press/2008/05/20/the-girl-who-struck-out-babe-ruth/

Schudel, Matt. "Dorothy "Dottie" Kamenshek dead; women's professional baseball player." *Washington Post.* May 22, 2010.
http://www.washingtonpost.com/wp-dyn/content/article/2010/05/21/AR2010052104773.html

Schwartz, Larry. "Didrikson was a woman ahead of her time." ESPN.com.
https://espn.go.com/sportscentury/features/00014147.html

Stewart, Sara. "Will a woman ever play in the major leagues?" *New York Post,* August 23, 2014. http://nypost.com/2014/08/23/will-a-woman-ever-play-major-league-baseball/

Toni Stone biography
http://www.biography.com/people/toni-stone-40319

GLOSSARY

amateur (AA-muh-chur)—A person who does an activity without being paid.

analytical (an-ah-LIH-tih-kul)—Able to clearly think through problems.

Cy (SIE) **Young Award**—A yearly award given to the top pitcher in Major League Baseball's American and National League.

documentary (dah-kyoo-MEN-tuh-ree)—A movie that records what really happened, such as the history of a country or the life of a person.

dominate (DAH-mih-nayt)—To win more than not.

influential (in-floo-EN-chul)—Having the power to cause change.

Instagram (IN-stuh-gram)—An online application that allows users to post short videos with text.

kinetic (kih-NEH-tik) **linking**—Using the entire body in a movement, such as throwing a baseball or running. The end result is more power.

Little League World Series—A yearly competition between the best youth baseball teams (ages 11 to 13) from all over the world.

Macy's Thanksgiving Day Parade—A huge parade through New York City that is shown on television throughout the country.

Major League Baseball Hall of Fame— A museum in Cooperstown, New York, that contains photos, displays, and more about the great players, managers, games, and records in baseball history.

memorabilia (meh-mor-uh-BEE-lee-uh)—Items or tokens that remind people of great people or events.

NBA (National Basketball Association)—The highest professional basketball league in North America for male players.

NCAA (National Collegiate Athletic Association)—The organization that oversees college sports.

poised (POYZD)—To be calm, composed, and polite.

professional (proh-FESH-uh-nul)—A person who is paid for doing sports or other activities.

tweet—A short message sent through the Internet site Twitter.

WNBA (Women's National Basketball Association)—The highest level of basketball in the United States for female players.

PHOTO CREDITS: P. 12—Point Blank Sports; p. 13—Imskinnynowwhat.com, p. 18—Sole Addicted; p. 18—Bleedphilly.com; p. 22—Jon Phenomenon, p. 26—Bob n Renee; all other photos—CreativeCommons. Every measure has been taken to find all copyright holders of material used in this book. In the event any mistakes or omissions have happened within, attempts to correct them will be made in future editions of the book.

INDEX

Anderson Monarchs 9, 10

Auriemma, Geno 19, 20

Bandura, Scott 19

Bandura, Steve 9, 10, 11

Beard, Hilary 21, 28

Beyoncé 13

Bloomsburg University 5, 6

Bush, Tim 11

California Angels 16

Casselberry, Joey 5, 6, 7

Cooperstown, New York 20, 31

Davis, Lamar 9

Davis, Mo'ne 4, 5, 6, 7, 8, 9, 10, 11, 13, 14, 15, 16, 17, 19, 20, 21, 23, 24, 25, 26, 27

Durant, Kevin 16

Fallon, Jimmy 18, 19

George Washington University 17

Griner, Brittney 19

HarperCollins Children's Books 21, 28

Hart, Kevin 23, 24

Hyman, Mark 17

Jeter, Derek 17

Kershaw, Clayton 19

Lamade Stadium 13, 17

Las Vegas 6, 17

Lee, Spike 20

Los Angeles Dodgers 19

Manning, Peyton 9

McCutchen, Andrew 16

McLean, Lakeisha 9

Moore, Maya 19

Newark, New Jersey 11

Obama, Barack 21

Obama, Michelle 20, 21

Papelbon, Jonathan 15

Philadelphia 5, 9, 11, 13, 15, 19

Rice, Alex 15, 16

Soltz, David L. 6

SportsKid of the Year 5, 20

Springside Chestnut Hill Academy 11

Taney Dragons 11, 15, 17, 20, 27

Taurasi, Diana 19

Trout, Mike 16

Washington Nationals 19

Williams, Mark 9

Williamsport, Pennsylvania 11, 13

Wooden, John 20